DIFFERENT & ALIKE

written by Nancy P. McConnell
illustrated by Nancy Duell

 Current®

Different & Alike
Printed in the United States of America
© 1982, 1988 Current Inc., Colorado Springs, Colorado 80941
*All rights reserved, including the right of
reproduction in whole or part.*

Library of Congress Catalog Card Number:
87-73309
ISBN 0-944943-00-4

What if everyone you knew were exactly like you? What if they had the same color of hair, the same color of eyes and they were just exactly your size? What if they even liked all the same things you liked—the same TV shows, the same games and the same kind of jelly on their peanut butter sandwiches? If people were all this much alike, it would be a pretty boring world!

Luckily, we are not all the same. Some of us are taller than others. Some of us are fat. Some of us are thin. Most of us wish we were something other than what we are at least some of the time. You may have lots of freckles while your brother has none. The boy who sits in front of you in school may be able to wiggle both of his ears while you can't wiggle even one. But you may be able to whistle much better than he can.

He can wiggle both of his ears!

3

duell

Because we are not all exactly alike, we say we are "different." Being different is only another way of being you. You should feel very special when you realize that no one else in the world is exactly like you!

Some differences are greater than others. Your skin may be black, white, brown or yellow—and you notice it's different from someone else's skin. Your family may go to church on Sunday while your neighbor's family goes on Saturday. That's a difference in religion. If you say

Being different is just another way of being you.

"y'all" (it rhymes with "ball") and your friend says "you guys," that could mean you come from different parts of the country. Someone who comes from a foreign country would speak even more differently than you!

The important thing to remember about all these differences is that the differences make us who we are. And having different people in the world is what makes it an interesting place to live. You should feel very special knowing you are one of a kind!

SOME DIFFERENCES
ARE CALLED HANDICAPS

Sometimes you may see or meet someone who is different because he or she has a handicap (it rhymes with "dandy cap"). A handicap is a difference which makes it harder for that person to do something which is easy for you to do—something like walking, seeing, speaking or hearing. People who are handicapped know they have this difference. They also hope you will feel it's no more important than any of the other things about them which make them different from you. Just like you, they have many likes and dislikes. Just like you, some things are hard for them to do while they can do other things very easily. And just like you, they want to be liked for who they are when *all* their differences are added together.

When we don't know all there is to know about something different, we are sometimes afraid of it. You may be afraid of a person's handicap because you don't understand it, or because it makes that person look or act a strange way. You may even worry that the handicap could be catching! Well, it isn't. It's only different.

All of us know how it feels to be handicapped in some way, if even for a short time. Have you ever been blind-

You were "blind" for awhile.

folded to play "Pin the Tail on the Donkey"? If so, you were "blind" for awhile. Have you ever sprained your ankle or broken your leg? If so, you were "physically challenged" for awhile. Have you ever tried to hear what someone was saying to you from the other side of a glass window but couldn't? Then you were "deaf" for awhile.

The examples we just mentioned are temporary, meaning that sooner or later they will go away. But some people have handicaps all the time—differences in how they learn, see, hear or move about that will never go away. Because the handicap will not go away, the person who has it must learn more about how to live with it.

First, they must try to understand why they have the handicap. Were they born with it, or was it caused by some

Handicapped people try to learn all about their handicaps.

accident or illness? What things can they still do? What things will be harder for them to do because of the handicap? Once they know the answers to these questions, they can begin to learn how to do some of the things their handicap makes it hard for them to do in a new way. After awhile, most handicapped people realize there is still so much for them to learn, experience and feel that having the handicap doesn't really matter so much after all.

BEING DEAF

If you were watching television and something suddenly happened to the sound, you would be very upset and frustrated, wouldn't you? Part of the enjoyment of watching your favorite program would be gone, because you would no longer be able to hear what was happening. However, soon you would stop worrying about hearing and you would try to figure out what was happening in other ways. You would watch what the people were doing and the expressions on their faces. Maybe you would even watch their lips to see if you could figure out what they were saying. Deaf people do these things, too.

People who are not totally deaf may be called "hearing impaired." They may hear some sounds well, but need help hearing other sounds. Or they may hear better when sounds are louder. Just as many people who don't see well wear glasses, many people who don't hear well wear small, electronic devices called "hearing aids" to help them hear better. Many people who wear hearing aids still have trouble hearing speech. People who cannot hear at all or are hearing impaired may need to learn new ways to communicate.

When people can no longer hear with their ears, they learn to "hear" by using their eyes. With their eyes they

If something suddenly happened to the sound, you would be very upset!

dvell

can tell what you are saying by "reading" your lips. Talk to your friends by moving your lips without making a sound. Can they understand what you are saying? If so, then they are reading your lips.

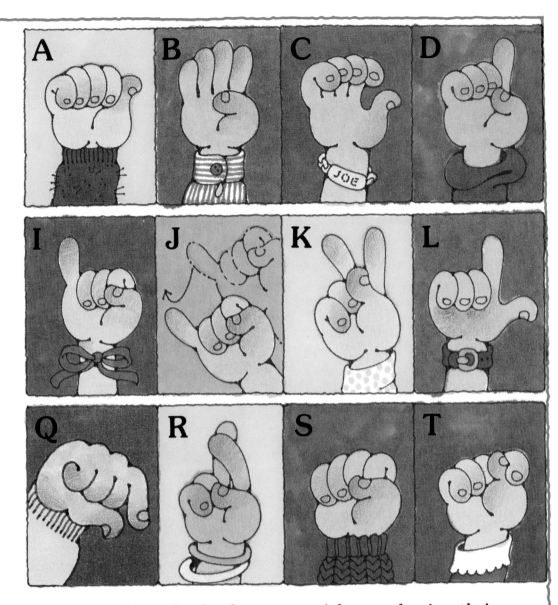

Deaf people also have a special way of using their hands to "talk" to each other. The "manual alphabet" shown here has a hand sign for every letter of the alphabet. Notice how some of the signs look very much like the letter they represent.

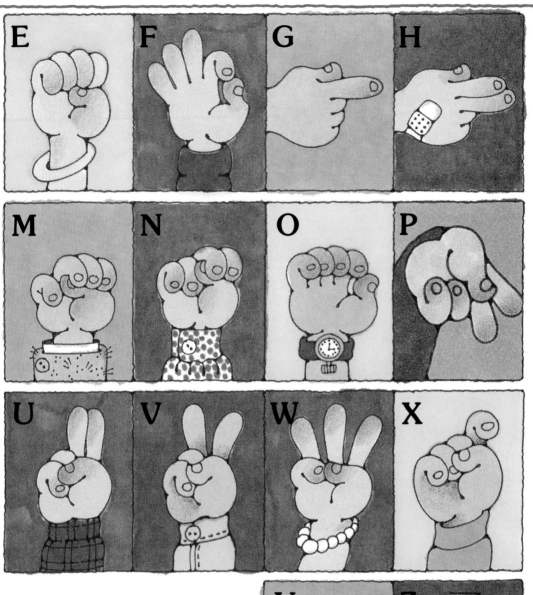

Using this guide, you can spell anything you want to say with your hands. Practice saying something to a friend.

Because it takes so long to spell out words letter by letter, however, there is also a system of hand signing in which one sign stands for a whole word, phrase or emotion. You "talk" like this every day without even knowing it!

If a player on your school's basketball team scores a winning goal, do you put your hands in your pockets or clap them together? If you are telling your mom you have a stomachache, do you hold your head or your stomach? If you are angry, is your hand clenched in a fist or waving? See, you use sign language too! Practice making the signs in this book. Then think about how many other signs you know.

Signing is especially important to people who have never been able to hear, as they often have trouble learning to speak. Babies learn to talk by repeating what they hear. People who can't hear often talk differently because they can't hear themselves or others speak.

You use
sign language too!

I love you.

Thank you.

Help you?

Friend

15

In addition to hearing aids, other special tools are used to help people who are hearing impaired. A special telephone, which includes a keyboard like a typewriter and a computer-type screen, allows two people who can't hear over a regular telephone to send messages to one another. A special "decoder," which may be attached to a regular TV, allows people who can't hear the sound to read the "closed captions" flashed on their screens. Dogs have been trained to help people who can't hear, too. They alert their masters when someone is at the door by touching them in a certain way. They are also trained to react to all kinds of danger, especially fire, in order to protect their masters.

Dogs alert their deaf masters when someone is at the door.

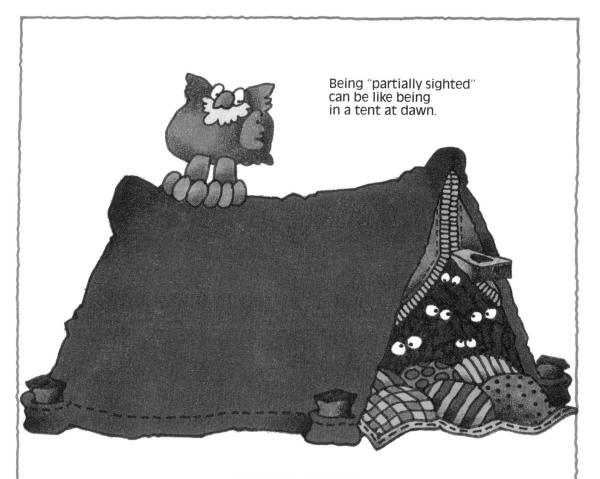

Being "partially sighted" can be like being in a tent at dawn.

BEING BLIND

Being totally blind is like always being in the dark, and it is a difference which takes quite a bit of adjustment. People who are not totally blind are called "partially sighted." Some of these people may be able to see things as long as they are very close. Others may only see shapes and shadows, sort of like being in a tent at dawn. Remember how we said deaf people learn to "talk" with their hands and "hear" with their eyes? Well, blind people learn to "see" using their other senses, too.

Have you ever gone to the museum or library where there is a "touch and feel" box? You can stick your hand into this box and feel things—like snakeskin, deer fur, or bird feathers—that you cannot see. You can't see these things with your eyes, but because you can feel them, you know what they are. You "see" them with your hands.

Even when we are tiny babies we learn about things by feeling them. Blind people learn many more things by feeling—even how to read!

Babies learn about things by feeling them.

The special system which was invented to help blind people read is called Braille (it rhymes with " sail "). Books which are printed in Braille have a series of raised dots which st and for c er - t a in letters and words. Did you feel the Braille on this p a g e as you were r ea d ing? I f not, go b a c k and " r ea d " it again with your f in ge rs .

Blind people have other special ways of doing things, too. They listen very carefully. By listening, they know when someone enters a room, or when the cars have stopped at the traffic light and it's safe to cross the street. They also memorize where everything is in their homes so they can move about freely and not bump into any of the furniture. Some blind people have special dogs, called "guide dogs," who can follow commands to guide their masters safely from place to place. These dogs actually become the "eyes" of their masters.

Blind people might also use canes to help them find their way from one place to another and as a sign to other people that they are blind.

Guide dogs become the "eyes" of their masters.

BEING DEAF AND BLIND

Some people are doubly handicapped because they are deaf *and* blind. This means they can't use their ears to help them "see" or their eyes to help them "hear." Even these people are able to communicate, however.

Many deaf-blind persons "hear" through palm printing or finger spelling. In palm printing, each letter in a word is traced in the palm of the deaf-blind person. Ask someone to write a secret message on your back with his or her finger. Can you figure out what they are saying? This is how palm printing works.

In finger spelling, the finger and knuckle positions of the manual alphabet are placed in the cupped hand of another person. In hand-on-hand signing, the person feels the hand of the person signing. Braille is also a big help to the deaf-blind person and, thanks to a new device, a punched tape of Braille can be sent from one person to another.

Ask someone to write a secret message on your back with her finger.

HAVING LEARNING DISABILITIES AND SPEECH DISORDERS

Think about how your mind differs from someone else's. You may be a real whiz kid in math, but just barely pass those weekly spelling tests. Maybe your sister asks you for help with her math homework every night, but always wins the spelling bee! You and your sister are different. You may have noticed that someone in your class needs more time to learn something new than the rest of the class does. This person may have a handicap called a "learning disability."

People with learning disabilities may look at the word "saw" and see the word "was" instead, because some words get turned around backwards in their minds. Or, they may see some letters differently—"nose" may look like "mose" for instance. That's why they have to try extra hard to learn to read. Sometimes they get very frustrated. It's not really helpful to tell people with learning disabilities to hurry up, because they are probably doing the best they can. Special teachers can help these people adapt to their handicap in time. It just takes lots of patience.

We all know someone who stutters, lisps, or has other trouble speaking clearly. This person may have a "speech disorder." People with "language disorders" may have a problem saying what they are thinking. By working with a special teacher called a "speech and language pathologist," children and adults can often adapt to their speech or language disorders and learn to communicate more clearly.

You and your sister are different.

BEING PHYSICALLY CHALLENGED

Have you ever stubbed your toe or stepped on a bee when you were barefooted and had to hop all the way home on one foot? Did you ever run in a potato relay with one arm tied behind your back? Then you have some idea how it feels to be "physically challenged."

Physical challenges are handicaps which are usually easy to notice. Someone who is physically challenged may be in a wheelchair, on crutches, wear a brace, or have an arm or leg missing.

People with physical challenges must learn to be very clever and develop new ways to do the things they used to do more easily. For instance, did you ever think about how a person in a wheelchair would get dressed? Sit in a chair in front of your closet and think about how you would reach your clothes. Soon you would invent a tool to help you, wouldn't you?

Luckily, many special tools and many kinds of special equipment have been invented to help people with physical challenges—including artificial arms, legs, hands and feet! Computers are used more and more to help people communicate or to perform certain tasks for them. Some computers can even react to the sound of the human voice.

Soon you would invent
a tool to help you.

Look around in your school or in the building where you shop or live to see how many things have been changed to help physically challenged people. Is the drinking fountain lower? Is there a railing in the bathroom? You have probably noticed specially marked parking spaces for handicapped people, too. These spaces are close to the building to make it easier for physically challenged people to get in and out.

Thanks to a group called Helping Hands, small monkeys have been trained to help many physically challenged people. These monkeys are especially helpful to quadriplegics, people without use of their arms and legs. They can turn the pages of a book, change TV channels, bring beverages or food, or do just about anything their masters direct them to do. Like guide dogs, they also make great friends!

Monkeys can be both entertaining and helpful!

BEING MENTALLY HANDICAPPED

When the differences that exist in someone's brain are great enough to keep that person from learning and growing normally, we say the person with that difference is mentally handicapped. One serious kind of mental handicap is "mental retardation."

Most mentally retarded people, about eight out of every ten, are only "mildly retarded" and can learn almost everything you can learn when they receive special instruction. Some of them are "severely retarded," however, and may have to be cared for by other people all their lives.

A common cause of mental retardation is a condition called "Down's syndrome." Since one out of every 650 babies born may have this condition, the chances are pretty good that you may know someone with Down's syndrome. If so, you know that although people with this condition look different, many of them are able to learn in the classroom and to compete in all sorts of physical activities.

The human brain has been called the world's first computer. The nerves in our brains are like wires in the computer, and our brain cells are like the computer's "memory." Information travels through our brains much like it does through a computer. The brains of mentally

The human brain was the first computer.

handicapped people may be like computers which aren't working correctly. Messages may not always be received or transmitted as clearly as they are by a brain that is working well.

We need to remember that while mentally handicapped people may not be able to do everything everyone else can do, they *can* do many things well. In spite of their differences, they can be loving friends to those who try to understand them.

BEING EMOTIONALLY HANDICAPPED

Emotionally handicapped people are those who have fears or feelings which can keep them from doing the things they want to do. They may sometimes have trouble getting along well with other people or may seem unhappy more than most people. They may also get frustrated very easily.

Emotionally handicapped people may feel as if they are on a roller coaster they can't control. Sometimes they will be "up" and sometimes "down," but they don't know exactly when the change will happen or how fast they will be going when it does! Emotionally handicapped people are not able to change their behavior easily. They need our understanding and support.

Emotionally handicapped people may feel as if they are on a roller coaster.

HELPING A HANDICAPPED PERSON

Remember how we said all people are different, and having a handicap is just one kind of difference? Knowing that is true is the best way to help a handicapped person, but there are other ways, too. When you are with a totally deaf person, remember that shouting really won't do any good—it will only make you red in the face and give you a sore throat! Instead, make sure you are looking directly at the deaf person when you talk and you are speaking as clearly as possible. Then it will be easy for the person to read your lips. Use as much sign language as possible, using your hands and your body, even if you don't know the manual alphabet or the official signing system. Remember, some signs are easily understood by everyone!

If you know someone who is blind, remember that being blind is only one difference. A blind person can usually hear perfectly well, so don't ask someone else how blind people feel or what they want to do—ask them! If you are eating dinner with a blind person, tell him or her about the food. It is helpful to ask the person to think of the dinner plate as a clock. Then you can say, "Your meat is at 2:00 and your potatoes are at 4:30!" It may be helpful for you to guide a blind person, but make sure you ask first if your help is needed. Sometimes blind

Shouting will only make you red in the face!

people feel they are being pushed or pulled around like a lawn mower or something! That really doesn't feel very helpful. You can be a "sighted guide" for the blind by allowing them to hold on to you. They will know when to go and when to stop by sensing your movement.

The best way to help a person with a learning disability or a speech disorder is to be patient. Don't try to do the reading or the speaking for the other person. Of course, it's never helpful to laugh *at* a person with a learning disability or any kind of handicap, but it is often helpful to laugh *with* that person!

People who are physically challenged will sometimes need your help to open a door, cross a street, or maybe even to eat or drink.

To be a friend to people who are mentally or emotionally handicapped, encourage them to do their very best at all the things they can do. You can help them find out what they do best by letting them try to do everything you can do.

Whenever you want to help any handicapped person, first ask how you may help or if your help is needed at all. You don't want to do something for your friend that he or she is proud of being able to do alone. We all know how frustrating that can be. When in doubt about how to help anyone, try giving them a hug. We can all use more of those!

People who have handicaps
will sometimes need your help.
Always ask first.

Most importantly, remember that all handicapped people are like you in more ways than they are different. Just like you, they can do some things better than others. Just like you, they have lots of different feelings. They can feel happy, sad, excited, frustrated, proud, lonely and loved—just like you. After all, we are all more alike than different.

INDEX

(continued on next page)

INDEX *(continued)*